Gallery Books
Editor Peter Fallon

MOCKER

David Wheatley

MOCKER

Gallery Books

Mocker
is first published
simultaneously in paperback
and in a clothbound edition
on 26 October 2006.

The Gallery Press
Loughcrew
Oldcastle
County Meath
Ireland

www.gallerypress.com

ISBN 1 85235 402 X *paperback*
1 85235 403 8 *clothbound*

ISBN 978 1 85235 402 2 *paperback*
978 1 85235 403 9 *clothbound*

A CIP catalogue record for this book
is available from the British Library.

Contents

MOCKER

City

I seem to have found my level:
        flat, all is flat, from the moment
you come off the ring road, leaving
        behind the bridge
and the estuary's curled lip
        chewing on Lincolnshire:
nothing rises,
        nothing will rise,
the few stumps of churches
        and tower blocks have stood
to regret their misjudgement;
        stealthy tenfoots and avenues
fall away under your feet
        into gaps in the clay
and speluncular drains;
        inch by inch
terraced hutches subside
        among the Bingo halls
and industrial estates,
        or, if they hold on, cling
to each other for neither
        warmth nor protection
(habit is too strong a word),
        and only a rare tabby
ventures out through a flap
        to bask on a bin lid,
as if for collection, though someone
        must live here, the teenagers
disappearing down
        the embankment or slouched
in the tattooist's door
        eyeing the line of unfortunates,
the dispersed ones, queuing

on sufferance for
their coupons and stamps,
the veteran shuffling
from the post office under
their empty gaze;
once all this was rubble,
the nostalgia freesheet
will tell you, rubble
and death where you're standing,
the people never happier,
useless to try to explain,
the dust of sixty years
slowly settling on our eyelids
as we blink at our good fortune,
pushing open the front door
we never bother to lock,
raising one foot above the other
at the foot of the stairs and already
standing on top of the world.

The Cold

There is little landscape where you are going and no warmth.

But for the cold sealing the estuary in
behind the fish market, behind the bridge-view car park,
so that the sharp air smells only of us,
would it be easier or harder to feel ourselves
marked by these afternoons we shoulder like a hand-me-
down coat?

The man on the corner stoops to coax a pigeon
into his outstretched hands, straightens up, claps them
to warm himself, applauding the street theatre
of his failure as the bird waddles free
(there will be more time to waste where that came from),

the weather hardening round us, my hand inside
the lagging jacket in an upstairs flat
feeling the cylinder cold. We will have to be patient,
as the hatchbacks that ease over the avenue
speed bumps are patient, the children in the back seats

staring up at us unfathomably
distant and content. The January sun
releases its grip on the day and my hand slips under
the cardigan sleeve you wouldn't have pulled down
to clutch in your palm so tightly but for the cold.

Riptide

When the Hawk jet came down in the Humber, bedding
down with the dogfish and Roman remains,
you could point to your rush of foreboding
when it flew over, showing the strain

in the sub-concert pitch timbre of
its rip-roaring bark and ominous height
above our lately re-pointed roof
that would have passed briefly through its sights,

sights that would soon zero in on the river,
its sluggish affront to such predatory grace,
the foul-mouthed gulls well below radar
and the sudden allure of losing all trace

of its own radar trace in one last kill —
itself — in the parting tide for the Hawk
supreme in the air even now in its fall,
the pilot shot free like a champagne cork.

Bankside-Wincolmlee by Instamatic

homage to Peter Didsbury

'Making a work is not thinking thoughts but accomplishing an actual journey.'
— David Jones, *The Anathémata*

1

Do they all lift, all these bridges, even this far up the river? Picture it unstitched the whole of its length, like a gutted haddock. Behind B&Q three teenage boys are fixing their lines and casting into the puddle of sludge between the river's cowpat banks. Who shall have a fishy?

2

The tipped cigar of the chimney shifts from side to side of the river, depending how far along the road you are. Keep an eye on it.

3

Empty yard, school of disused branch railway line. A memory of Foxrock-Boghill railway station one Sunday drive, everything covered in awnings, huge heavy white awnings. Then gone the next time. A bicycle against a wall that would seem to suggest habitation.

4

Closer into the yard, following the line of the sprayers' tags, their autopsy report on the place recording an open verdict.

5

I do not know which to prefer, the beauty of inflecting the chimney from yet another angle, its bluntly Up-yours verticality when it comes into view, or just after. On balance the 'Up-yours' has it.

6

The yard warehouse, from a broken window further along the road: the factory floor of urban anti-matter.

7

You will *not* drive your car down this alley for dumping in the river. Show some respect.

8

You will dump your car here instead, but only when you've burnt it out first. This can be arranged.

9

An eighteenth-century graveyard, never very energetically used ('a few more widows' and they'll be turning them away), the locals too lazy to die in any great numbers.

10

A car battery of a mill, other side of the river from behind a high wall, narrow corridor of a road, lorries thundering past, the A in a circle on their bonnets just like the one I used to play with in my back garden twenty-five years ago: just like the A in the circle I used to see on the back of parka jackets. A for Atkinson, A for anarchy.

11

The chimney from the bank, definitely on the other side this time, the river threading itself through the eye of the needle's reflection.

12

Exquisite pagoda on stilts sitting on top of the red corrugated iron bridge, a vase of flowers in the window, their preposterous red, lipstick on a mannequin thrown in a skip.

13

Trying, trying, almost, but not quite catching it, the stunning bulk of the mill's bid for escape velocity, upward, skyward. Back you step another twenty paces and try again.

14

This one easily the best of the lot: the stubble of grass at your feet, the mudbanks, the chimney left corner, the mill released into blue where the fire escape (it's not a fire escape, is it?) frames its failure of will in an airborne empty door, that ecto-plasmic wisp of cloud over all, perfect.

15

On to the working yards and 'Advertise here' hoardings, advertisements for advertisements, the turn for the bargain hotel, the café we will charitably assume is only closed for lunch, cars parked in the street, signs of activity everywhere. Activity? There goes the neighbourhood!

16

The old Gospel Hall's pediment has awarded itself, at its apex, the tribute of a scraggy wreath. Let the gospel according to Hot Booze Cash and Carry be observed by all who pass this way. Could this be 'an Arctic kind of Xanadu', 'a case of etcetera etcetera?', the ghost of William Cowper flitting by?

17

Signs of life about another brown mill: 'An industry already comatose, / Yet sparsely living.'

18

A bend in the river, heavy and lutulent: the fetid brown gums of the Hull bared in a vacant smile, the predator briefly at rest, wondering where its next meal will come from.

19

What if not time itself are the warehouses storing down another Utrillo-meets-Lowry windowless street?

20

Here in the empty heart of the city, intangibly within sight by now, the image of the king reproduces a 'portraicture of his sacred majestie' along these warehouse rooflines, imprinting the stigmata of his infinite 'solitude and sufferings' on every spike of this yellow security fence.

21

A pub: The Whalebone. In *Moby-Dick* Melville describes the skeleton of a sperm whale washed up on the North Sea coast and claimed by the Lord Paramount of the Seigniory of Holderness: 'Sir Clifford's whale has been articulated throughout; so that like a great chest of drawers, you can open and shut him, in all his boney cavities — spread out his ribs like a gigantic fan — and swing all day up on his lower jaw. [. . .] Sir Clifford thinks of charging twopence a peep at the whispering gallery in the spinal column; threepence to hear the echo at the hollow of his cerebellum; and sixpence for the unrivalled view from his forehead.'

22
Or was it him after all? Steady yourself against the brief blue railing, its reassuringly end-of-the-banister, cast-iron solid globe.

23
The bridge thrown open on its massive hinges, impassive leviathan sieving the plankton of low tide, you the one shrimp swimming downstream that will have got away.

24
Or has he escaped? The mudbanks' gingivitis assumes a terminal air. Once I would have been doing this every other day, or night: now I hardly know my way round. *You're a big man, but you're out of shape. With me it's a full-time job. Now behave yourself.*

25
Seen from between the blue 'boney' cavities of the bridge, the last outcrop of mills before the flood barrier and the river spilling its guts into the Humber.

26
And the image of the king shall be known as 'Eikon Basilike', to whom all hail. All hail his sovereign territories and subjects: the Zoo café, bargain shops on Newland Avenue, a pair of axolotls in the Pearson Park conservatory and its whistling rosella, Sam the swearing macaw, the pavement fish alphabet, cats down tenfoots, the ducks of Westbourne Avenue and someone's pet sheep (heard but never seen), potato groupers and slate-grey wrasse trailing the broken matchstick of their barbels in The Deep. The last stretch of the riverbank awaits

his majesty's pleasure, a leisurely stroll to the estuary and the cosy glow of all the departing ferries he will never take.

27

After the last bridge's cage bars the river becomes its banks, mudbanks ascendant, supreme, the sky wispless, all else buried, face down in the shit the vision at last: drowning, drowned, perfect.

Stan

Stan: the bouquets in the window
spell his name. He is turning
the corner, out of view,

as I press for the traffic to stop,
four black cars slinking
behind him. The hearse pulls up.

Stan, though he has an appointment, has time.
I signal discreetly, *wouldn't you rather . . .*
sure of what feels like a rule of thumb

until the driver uncurls his fist
and extends a finger politely
demanding *you go first.*

The Gas Mask

If I still had the use of my mind I'd call it insane.
When I got in the taxi he took me, as we drove home,
on a detour through a pet theory of his
that went something like: *Cells of them, one big plot,*
already over here, anthrax, Saddam, our boys,
only language he understands, gas attack,
one in the attic, my grandad's, Geiger counter . . .

After which the next thing I heard was a grunt, or
was it me slithering down the seat in the back?,
then a honk rocking the cab with the noise
as he turned and a pendulous, rubber snout
loomed at me from his wall-eyed elephant's face:
he'd already put it on and I had to tell him,
'Sorry, I can't understand a word you're saying.'

Sonnet

stretch pants	cashback	pound shop	store card
hubcaps	tailfin	souped-up	Escort
breakbeat	ringtone	dole day	cheques cashed
loan shark	small change	rat boys	bag snatched
tin can	tomcat	backstreet	dosshouse
TV	late lunch	warmed-up	Chinese
black dog	tongue stud	real nails	fake tan
red light	road rage	brain-dead	Leeds fan
handbrake	wheelspin	pub crawl	big screen
spiked drink	lift home	knocked up	sixteen
knocked up	knocked out	well gone	all gone
all day	all week	stay home	what's on
chat shows	pig out	hard stuff	hard case
hard luck	fuck life	fuck off	now please

Diamonds

Diamonds are this girl's
best friend, one beaming
from her midriff,
its fashion statement rife
in this twin town of Freetown,
Sierra Leone.
Children of Freetown,
diamond town,
your cries on a loop
in the slave museum:
shine as it will,
the beam in my eye
refracts through a dark
more dazzling still.
Disarmingly so,
children of Freetown,
stump town:
forgive us the hands
that give to collectors,
forgive us who do
and do not know better,
our jeweller's shop
where the belly-pierced girl
will stop to look,
the stone in her navel
a harmless fake
dazzling its
transparent rebuke
as I follow her down
Freetown way,
her vanishing form
a mote in my eye.

The Owl

after Baudelaire

Owl at my window, window owl,
under the sycamore's midnight eaves,
alien god whose red eye roves
while he sits tight and plays it cool.

No police copter or car alarm
can budge him from his airy perch,
unflappable, who must keep watch
until the hour of perfect calm.

Look and learn: don't just do
something, stand there! Stand still and be wise.
Be the owl who does as he pleases.

Drunk on every passing shadow
man will always pay the price
for having wanted to change places.

The Literary Life

This year's prize
for best collection

by a squirrel
goes to

the squirrel
in my back garden

for his outstanding
collection, *My Nuts*.

(There he goes now
on the fence
with a new one.)

In their citation
the judges wrote,
'This is an outstanding
collection of nuts,

witty but true,
dazzling but wise,
delicate but tough.

This is a collection
of nuts

(unless he eats them of course)

we'll be returning to
for many years to come.'

Macaw

Because the terrible hook-nosed scarlet macaw
will not leave me in peace I bring him tributes
of sliced fruit he scatters in raucous disdain,
whistle him tunes he knows far better than I,
begin sentences he interrupts
to finish. Because he will as soon
have my eyes out as look at me
through the swivelling molluscs of his own
I cower and will myself small as the ripple
I make in his darting, aqueous humour
but in he dives after me into the black
pool of his stare and will not rest until
his maggot tongue has slimed the hand
he perches atop and he has trodden hand,
shoulder and head beneath his standstill march
and opened his wings over my head
to stand for a moment, the terrible wingspan
doing its clipped, furious worst as I cower
and cover my eyes in the black shadow
of every last scarlet, blue and green feather
and 'Help!' try to shout, dummy to his ventriloquist,
'Help!', and screeching he interrupts me
for the whole street to hear, 'Help, help, help!'

Axolotl

Ambystoma mexicanum

All the blood has drained from my face.
Arrowheads of Canada geese convey
formation victory signs to the shivering
pond this winter Sunday, and within
our indoor park, the misting-over-
before-my-glasses conservatory,
the rosella whistles 'Pop Goes the Weasel'
and two axolotls squirm in their tank
beside the piranhas as though fresh woken
from the formaldehyde surprise
of survival through geological time,
the years of hoarding their Aztec god
of a name under a stone. Notable for their
'permanent retention of larval features,
such as external gills', and also for
their black eyes, not red: not alibied
by a truant pigment but thus by design.
Rhythmically the anemone ruffs fan out,
batting at us but non-flirtatious:
they will not mate, not with our gaze
and not with each other, but celebrate
their pyrrhic victory, pyrrhic defeat,
as best they know how. They hang
in the water, borne along on the tank's
absent ripples, passing each other like
waterborne toys, dangling mobiles.
Evolve or die! Or: fail to evolve
and survive just the same! — And at night,
hoisted on their pudding hind legs
they rattle the locked conservatory door
for as long as their held breath lasts

and slouch back to their tank to weigh it all up:
the evolving or dying, the dying or surviving,
the evolving or dying or staying the same —
decisions, decisions — these millions of years.

Sloth

'My absolute favourite piece of information is the fact that young sloths are so inept that they frequently grab their own arms and legs instead of branches, and fall out of trees.'

— Douglas Adams

Arm raised, matted compost basket
hung from his billhook toes, the stupidest boy
in the class has a question. Why does the bum-faced
monkey throw its poo? The yahoos storm
up and down and drum hello on the glass.
Incandescent, temperate, tepid, frozen
over with rage, bemusement, indifference —
sorry, what was it again? — the perfectly empty
head retracts into its algal carpet.
There are few activities for which the crown
of a palm tree can be improved on: eating,
sleeping, giving birth, watching a youngster
take a coconut plunge to the forest floor
where he can watch him slowly die rather than:
no, he can't be bothered. His tree-high
ancestors had neither occasion nor
the capacity for life upside down, for which
ill-judged uprightness extinction swiftly,
or rather slowly, very slowly followed.
In static alliance with the coelacanth
and giant tortoise our strap-hanging friend
has rendered extinction redundant. Henceforth
let all our aspirations to rise be upside
down and flying poo the fastest thing
to trouble our sight. Arm still raised, he has
a question he has long, long since forgotten:
If I raise my arm to grip the branch which is
my arm, release my arm to grip the same arm,

what am I lacking to hold myself up? Am I
not there
to catch myself
as I fall?

Edward Delaney, 'The Gymnast'

Our first night,
I miss the train home.
I knew that I would.
In search of a bed,
floor or mat
offering welcome,

find myself walking
(you are there too)
in D6,
the swing-gate creaking
as we stray into
your old college digs.

There in the garden
an acrobat hangs
from a high bar,
her ponderous burden
defying the air.
O high jinks!

She hangs, unmoving:
cast in steel.
How had I missed
your ghost of a smile
as I moved in
and we almost kissed?

Almost: not quite,
not yet, even if
I take sudden aim
at your front door mat,

still miles off,
flex my hams

and hightail
it, jumping for joy,
not stealing a glance
at the jury until,
both knees giving way,
I come in to land.

Complaint

'I by the tide of Humber . . .'

When you came back unannounced
from your fruitless Ganges cruise
my greeting was more like the moan
of a would-be dead ringer
for the lovelorn Yorkshireman,
to whose still-echoing cries
I decided to take my chance
and slip a ring on your finger.

Numerology

'The cartographer lists and draws fourteen bastions, fourteen wall-towers, fourteen main thoroughfares, fourteen monasteries, fourteen castles, fourteen laneways . . .'

— James Joyce, 'The City of the Tribes'

Purity of heart is to will one thing.
A pair of Trinity squares, down for the week:
how could that salty longing not awake
by Galway Bay, our hearts gone for a song?

Under the arch, over the Corrib, pent
in a guest house, working it out again, the six-
es and sevens of it, the algebra of sex,
the octopus arms and legs out for the count

come 'Breakfast at nine', at ten . . . Waking to
elevenses, a sleepy one on one,
we get up to the Angelus' round of applause,

the tilly of a kiss in the street: the two
of us in the city of fourteen tribes, awash
with fourteen shades of light that colour us one.

Galway, 1998

Gable End

'Tá Tír na nÓg ar chúl an tí . . .'
— Seán Ó Ríordáin

Their day never to come, they have gone to the wall.
Like holy beggars they seem to have lost all will.
Their love affair with the future has made them ill,

the people who speak neither English nor Irish
and stand the ground only they could cherish
by the gable end of the last house of the parish,

shouldering their burden not to be borne,
the people who are neither native nor foreign.
Somewhere among these streets my mother was born

and now I too return to prod at the past,
content if I can be the unnoticed guest
and drop dead letters to myself in the post,

delivered and thrown away at the gable end
as I must have been, to end up lost and found
sharing my postcode with the rain and wind.

I paint myself into the tightest corner
and, though I could not be a slower learner,
mouth the slogans on each flag and banner

that I might join the gable end people
at last, surrendering to their appeal
and saying a prayer beneath their dreary steeple,

though they believe in neither Church nor God
but only the straw on which they make their bed,
outcast on the world. Yet they seem glad.

And we too are glad, making ourselves at home
among the averted gaze, the grating hymn,
the shout in the backstreet, the sanctified harm,

the shopping centre and the tourist trail:
security discreet; all of it real,
only our appetite for it still on trial,

and the signs in which we saw it all foretold —
Quis Separabit, What We Have We Hold —
urgently redundant, self-fulfilled

like us and fading as we lose all will,
our day come and gone, the pair of us still
with nowhere to shelter but this gable wall.

A Backward Glance

He mishears 'Yorkshire':
dhearcas siar.
His own small teary
Dialann Deoraí.

Bempton

In past centuries it was believed that migrating birds would winter on the moon.

Because there is always another sea to cross,
each sanctuary a new departure lounge,
they will not come and join us in the grass
but, magnetized by its silver grey, plunge

their jokers' beaks into the killing tide
and come away mock-whiskered with their catch
(their flying style is staggering, their trade
a roaring one, with a deft side-splitting touch).

Your first time puffin-watching. I watch you chart
each flight path up and down the louvered cliff
amid the echoing guffaws, at mine

and your expense. And when the August lift-off
comes, and the cliff empties? Listen hard.
They're laughing still, on the far side of the moon.

Scrimshaw

I have stood by the pier so long
I am little more than quivering blubber,
though you'll bleed from me

no oil for the watchman's lamp,
no ambergris to smooth
these cracked cheeks over,

harpoon-widow, good
for a daguerreotype in my half-door
or leaving a fish-head out for the cat.

But spare me your genre pieces:
my worst imaginings dive deeper,
longer than any plankton-eater,

and cut like a flensing knife through bone,
my one good ear always cocked
for the house-high slap of the minke's tail

whiplashed along the Iceland current
past Whitby and Brid
to me, the whaler's mermaid wife

painting myself with a wig and an idiot grin
on a walrus tusk, for filing away
with the chess pieces and shaving sets,

reconciled to my years
as the accessioner's curio hostage,
second only in his affections

to the stuffed polar bear;
dependable as the foghorns
carrying from the estuary

again tonight —
like clock radios, you think,
turning over in bed,

sounding their wake-up call
over and over for an appointment
you will sleep through,

dead to the blood-red hours,
their promiscuous designs
on your eyelids, ghosting

my form there, like scrimshaw.

Cod Liver Oil

Hooking the Icelandic gunboat on the line
of the Humber we reeled it in to the quayside pub,
its covered guns a vision of prophylactic
civic goodwill. Its low note hung in the air

like tone-deaf echolocation or a sportive
call to ramming — that tug, that ferry — before
the minute's silence for the unknown North Sea cod.
A pavement fish A-Z (anchovy,

brill, catfish. . .) stood us down from dominion
over the waters and deeps to the Scrabble version
we played with their overfished, gutted ebb
(. . . X-ray, yawling, zander). A whale beached

on the East Coast shingle had thrashed for gawpers
on the regional news, and I felt my wrist tingle
with harpoon nostalgia, the sickly honesty
of a world where only what you watch die

do you eat. Netted, landed and smoked,
the North Sea had become aldermanic
finger food, a briny vestige for the local
press-pack at the public art unveiling,

sifted leavings in a boyhood bottle
of cod liver oil, its slow-decanting cure
more rancid than any ill health. Speeches made,
the bronze *Voyage* stood mooning the docks

from its plinth and dived back out to sea.
Paper boats, trawlers, car ferries, gunboats

launched in its wake would find the tide empty,
only the swimmer's copper green, sexless

limbs in their nets and its hooked lips mouthing
the deep's excuses: the voyage had become
its own quarry, caught. Departing, the gunboat's
fading note reached nothing and the echo of nothing

and low tide threw up a trail of cod liver oil.
The tensing before the dive was voyage enough
and still I could scarcely keep up. I grimaced, drank,
told myself I was feeling better already.

Trade Winds

A passing St Brendan traded a sign of the cross
for a native's airborne lump of burning slag
and pronounced Mount Hekla the gates of hell.
Fire is tree-foe, gleams-of-dread that other
fire called gold. Cut me, I bleed it, fire,
a lava-flood in every vein. Snorri
Sturluson traded a witch a rotten
flounder for the two extra letters of
the Icelandic alphabet, one symbolizing
hero renown, the other a reindeer's bladder
speared on a stick. I trade you an arctic fox
and a reindeer for a hollow great auk's egg.
Buried three months before the midwinter feast
a rotten shark is not to be sniffed at, and goes
down well with a little Black Death spirit.
When offered these dainties at my table
you will know better than to refuse, though
a stranger took hospitality from Greppur
the Grim and killed him afterwards in his sleep.
Flosi and Skarphedinn traded insults
at the Althing, but Gunnar and Njal
remained friends. And yet Gunnar died.
The chess players of Grimsey island
would fling themselves into the sea in ecstasies
of disgrace when defeated. Fischer and Spassky
traded pawns in Reykjavik, each rocking
back and forth in his chair 'like dead men dancing'.
The sea, that knows all about dead men,
traded Iceland the island of Surtsey
for an eruption that lasted four years
before cooling to basalt, lichen and moss.
Now, thinking better of it, Surtsey's tephra
covering is borne away on the breeze

and only the gates of hell themselves
reopened could make it return. Afloat
on the Blue Lagoon's volcanic waters,
I feel the underworld's hot breath on my ankles:
Won't you have me back, it asks?
I would not trade it for anything on earth.

St John and the Eagle

Lindisfarne Gospels

In the beginning was something
or other — what was it? The saint's
parchment is blank, but from
the badger's snout will come the hair

for the brush, from the calf's
martyred back the vellum,
from Ireland the adze-headed scribes,
their insular majuscules, the DNA

coils of frets, trumpets and key steps
weaving a carpet of pages for you
over the sands at low tide:
from gall and indigo the green

and blue of your tunic, from heliotrope
the pinks and purples, and wrought
to its uttermost lapis lazuli
from Badakhshan of the peaks

from which the eagle will swoop,
scattering doves as he goes.
Evangelist's bird, tired
of the easy kill, the flocculent hare

and deckchair legs of the deer
folding under a ton's *worth of rapt*
persuasion in its claw: from a thousand
yards up the eagle has spied

and will snatch from your hands
your book, leaving you only
a feather with which to scatter
and sow The Word in his

fugitive image, *imago aquilae*:
no sooner will you have finished
this page than talons will
puncture and carry it off.

Chemical Plant

'I am pure ohm.'

Seventies concept album cover:
green fields round the chemical plant,
a torch flared in the breeze's shiver,
all the crop circles you could want
and two smoke plumes that go on forever.

Wind down your window for a smell
of the muskily igniting beast:
exoskeleton, pure shell
of power that hides no pacing ghost
but only purely living steel

slicing through the riverside view.
Always there but never seen,
let all humanity be the few
hard-hatted shadows that we join
to work this chemistry we do

to feed the fire firing the hum
that rises snaking from each tower
and drives the chain reaction home
that surges when it finds us, lover,
and runs to ground through our pale flame.

Mocker

The beach's naked
then clothed again
maja,
white-into-brown,
brown-into-white
again mocha:
the waves' kiss
forever short
of the machair.

Magadh

Idir nocht
agus feistithe
tá an trá ina *maja,*
cúrach idir
bán agus donn
ar nós mocha,
póg na dtonn
gan teagmháil riamh
leis an machaire.

Uggool / Ug Umhaill

An Errancy

In Aughavannagh's blessed acre
never, I swore, would I forsake her

and so, forsaking her, I fled
across the hills to Kevin's Bed

and slept on rock and bled wild berries
onto my tongue on Camaderry

and just because I saw it run
followed a deer to Devil's Glen.

*

On Lough Nahanagan's monstrous shore
I vowed and wept and vowed no more

until the hillside opened up
to cover me and make it stop.

But even as I climbed and sat
astride the world my only thought,

astride Croghanmoira and Glencullen,
was, hourly, how much more I'd fallen.

*

On Tonelagee as eagles prowled
I lit a fire and crouched and quailed

between the waterfall and wood
and threw myself on you, my God,

to think I sank as low as pray
bare-naked to the empty sky

and sank to sleep beneath the pines
as needles chafed my bare behind.

*

On Luggala I heard the news,
oh boy, that it was time to choose

the straight or crooked path back home
and choosing neither chose to roam

across the gap beyond all reason,
out of love and out of season,

and coming to a clear stream fell
and bathed my face and drank my fill.

*

In Glenmalure of Fiach MacHugh
I pined in one last wood for you

and, growing tired, we pledged our troth
and laid our bodies in the earth

for all along I'd carried you,
or you had me for all I knew,

and still we lay. Our foes would hound us.
They'd come, they'd look. They'll never find us.

Nostalgia

Petrol-on-tarmac, salmon-and-blue-on-sable
evening sky where the Canada geese take flight
over the pier, a tethered goat and cabal
of roosters lifting their muezzin cries all night.

A man and his dog — always one man and his dog —
emerge from or is it fade into the mist
and walk like you the thin line of the dyke
that follows the foghorns all the way to the coast.

Two Iraq-bound squaddies rattle the pool balls
down the pub, war over who'll buy the beer,
the worst they'll face tonight for whom the bell tolls
the struggle to get their shout in at the bar.

Blacktoft docks bombed!, Lord Haw Haw crackled over
the airwaves six decades ago. Let more bombs
fall tonight: I give it all up, river,
jetty, me staggering from the pub, to the flames

if in return they grant me an azure-and-pink-
against-pitch-black sunset streaking the sky
behind the Ouse while the geese sleep on the wing
and one man and his dog walk lazily by.

Whalebone Haiku

Here time is a slow
log on the fire, and the whole
evening still to go.

Nunc est bibendum.
That's Latin for line up those
pints and upend 'em.

I'm beached on the bar,
a Whalebone whale. When it spouts
my blowhole spouts beer.

If you can read this through
your pint, you're running low.
Go top it up now.

God knows the *anno*
domini since someone last
played the piano.

Hit one you're okay,
two trebles good, three and you're
king of the oche.

Off Gerrard's forehead:
goal! Champ-i-ons. *The lads were*
really up for it!

A pub is a boat.
It sails on froth. Each pint pulled
helps keep it afloat.

My Arctic Corsair!
Be my first mate, I'll be your
two-day millionaire.

Tanked up on ardour,
I'll make you mine if you make
me your last order.

The Teardrop Explodes

Falco peregrinus

Why does the teardrop become a diamond?
Why does the diamond not hit the ground
at a hundred-and-eighty, two-hundred-and-fifty
miles an hour, one wing in front
                    and one behind?
The boy racer pulls up short
in the half-second before impact
and peppers the air with a shock of swallows
                    black as their fear.
The 'I' of his absent smoke trail plummets
like a thermometer off the scale,
                    icing over
the zero of failure no
                    rerun will assuage.
The god's-eye perspective has shrunk
                    to a pinprick, escape
velocity slowed to the twitch
                    of a nerve flaring
                    his claws in rage.
The escaping swallows haul their way up
a glassy surface of tiny
                    scratch after scratch.

Fintan and the Hawk of Achill

'Am seabhac a néad i n-aill.' / 'I am a hawk, my nest on a cliff.'

Before the flood

was Fintan

born of a day

with the hawk

and surviving the flood

changed to a salmon

an eagle

a hawk

and a man again

possessed of all wisdom

knowing all magic

and the history of Ireland

born of a day

with the hawk that

the bitterest

night in memory

took shelter in

an eagle's nest

killed its young

told the mother

returning

of a colder night yet

told her

disbelieving

go ask the blackbird

its perch bent in two

it had stood there so long

who said

go ask the stag

whose antlers could fence

a whole field

who said

go ask the blind salmon

frozen tight

in its pond

one Bealtaine Eve

who said

if I am blind

it is the work

of the hawk who pecked out

my eyes one night

bitterer even

than this

and is now in your nest

nest the eagle

returning

found empty of

the hawk

who meeting Fintan

the pair began

to collogue:

five thousand five hundred   I am   five thousand
five hundred years old

put in the shape   of a salmon each spring
by the Bann   the Suir   the Liffey   the Shannon
to suffer   stuck fast   in the ice   of Assaroe   of the seals
came   the hawk
that plucked out   my eye

I took your eye   it was I   took your eye

pulled out my eye   pulled out my eye
recompense me my eye

I might peck out the other

five hundred years   a blind salmon   fifty
an eagle   a hundred a falcon   and now what I was
if I am anything

From each of your twelve   sons on the battlefield
I plucked   hand   foot   or eye
bore off the hand   of the Tuatha Dé Danann's
High King
carrion bird to   Cúchulainn himself   feasting on
rivers of blood   from the spears
of Naisi   Conall   Fergus   Cúchulainn
whom wounded   in battle   I found
and perched   on his face   to peck out his eyes
felt his spear enter   my flesh
its barb   there yet   I who had
borne off   the bodies   of champions and heroes
piglets and boars   before Daithi went east
too weary   now   to lift up a blackbird
who have flown here   from the west
for your blessing   O Fintan
that I may return there   westward
my journey   to die there   tomorrow

O bird

I will travel

with you

we will fly

by the light

of the eye

you pecked out

and drink

from waters

that coursed

in the flood

we will die

on Achill

older together

than all

the world

and God and time

asking forgiveness

we will admit them

to the cold shelter

under your wings

Our Lady of Ardee Street

The convent hill
puffs out its chest
like a child on his First

Communion day,
a tatty rosette
on his lapel.

All my life
women have been
coming at me with pins.

And worse:
the wetted finger
pressed to my cheek.

When you stop combing my hair
I will stop hating you,

held by the scruff
of my tangles: *Daithi Lacha,*
Davy the Duck.

The acid-bath crackle
of my rasher for tea

remembers its pig.
The uproar of them,

you tell me, recalling,
out in the garden.

Sharpen the knives!
The eggs in the frying pan
stare, big-eyed, aghast.

Earlier still, the squeals
of me, held upside down

in the basin for a hairwash,
a wriggling *banbh*.

Those amniotic waters
I swam in, their

anemones of women's
fingers. And a most delicious,

nourishing and wholesome
food this infant

would have made too,
with a little more flesh on him.

Turn those rashers: get them
just right. And then an ice cream

from The Punnet
on the corner for afters,

Our Lady robbed of her
blue plastic crown

for a finger and thumb's
worth of blessing

as I run to get it, largesse
bled from a wound,

a hole in the head. A crown
is a hat that lets the rain in.

Let it rain holy water
and I will bring back

from the shop and feed
the whole family with

the squeal of an Ardee Street pig.

*

Our Lady of Ardee Street:

Mother most mild

Star of the Sea

hushed and insistent
your voice

mouthing urgent
indecipherable words

of promise and warning
solace and grief as you slip

into the waters blue
against white on your hem

your wedding dress trail
dissolving into the tide

a spume of holy water
washing back up thinking
the better of it
withdrawing again

a jellyfish
it pulses dissolves
and is gone

'I burn . . .'

after Valéry

I burn with a flame that's all my own, but freeze
when I see this brutal life and see it whole . . .
Sleep's the only time I reconcile
myself to the world in which I spend my days.

I drift out in a light, uneasy doze
and meet the day just gone there — on patrol
and ready, if bad dreams are on the prowl,
to repeat itself behind my sleeper's eyes;

enjoying itself so much that when I wake
I'm thrown like a corpse in the tide against the flesh;
and like a shell that echoes that ocean's plash

my ears ring with strange laughter and I ache,
on the furthest edge of wonderment, with doubt —
Am I awake or asleep, alive or dead?

Drift

In Whitby, through its gaping jaw,
I entered the whale, was swept from shore,

began to drift and smuggled my way
in a used coffin to Robin Hood's Bay,

my one endeavour to route my calls
through a satellite phone at Fylingdales

to where you stood on Whitby sands,
an ice cream cone in both your hands.

*

From Scarborough prom where donkeys roamed
I fled in a dodgem and made for home

until sparks flew and I came to grief
bumped up against Anne Brontë's grave,

and went to ground in a B&B,
where I watched the tide and bade goodbye

with a postcard and an unpaid bill
and jumped on a trawler, drifting still.

*

In Bempton of the guanoed cliffs
I lived on gulls' eggs and dry leaves,

the puffins made me a laughing stock
and heckled and pecked me off their rock

to Brid where I won you a teddy bear.
You get my drift. I was drifting far

but only in search of a tidal spate
to wash me up, washed up, at your feet.

*

In Withernsea, taking care to shun
a nightclub called *Oblivion*

I shaved on a wind farm's turbine blade
and watched the last of the coastline slide

to where land gave itself up for lost,
threw itself off itself in disgust,

on Spurn, long dreamt-of vanishing point,
end of the line, of the world: the end

*

of nothing, as it turned out. I went down
once, twice, thrice, and woke up thrown

on a beach that could only be Skegness.
All that coastal drift and mess

had merely relocated south.
I jumped back into the whale's huge mouth

to drift back north and start again.
You'd left me my ice cream. But you were gone.

Owls, Fort Paull

Slip from its glass case in Fort Paull
the salt cellar formed from a vertebra
of Charles I, shake over our tails
enough salt to stop us flying away

and make for the bunkers, the rabbit holes
sloping down to the estuary
where the Amsterdam ferry walks on water
past the chemical plant, the shipyard

and whitewashed lighthouse, electron storms
of swallows round its empty head —
and make for the bunkers, make for the underground
safe from our falconer's owls, *Bubo*

bubo and *Bubo bengalensis,*
facing all ways at once on a bin lid,
cannon or tank, their hairy feet's
fulvous designs on the titbits of chicken

we taunt them with from a hundred yards,
who duck past the Churchill Tea Rooms
as they rise and pursue, rise, pursue,
swoop and pounce, shifting awkwardly

on our wrists by the Home Guard display
(the soundtrack speaking the nation's name
to itself in an afternoon nap behind glass,
but hopeful of waking up before teatime),

gurgling, dancing and spinning their heads,
hanging upside down, jangling

their bells and knotting their jesses,
wanting more chicken, flapping their wings

and sidestepping with us the Civil War
re-enactments to duck down our bolt hole
at last, the Henry VIII bunker's
dank maw, its empty-eyed waxworks

and primal dungeon of Albion's beefy
monarch and executioner side by side
and in one: disjecta membra of his
sovereign power, vertebrae scattered

like dice, Saturn devouring his children;
and the owls still gurgling and dancing,
spinning their heads and wanting feeding,
barking and growling, birds of Minerva,

owls in the sarcophagus, storming
in its blank walls   and catching   one each
swallowing us   like bugs   to devour
and bring back up   our bones   as pellets

two compacted   tidy cairns
fragile   to the touch   and for grinding down
atom   by atom   to nothing   to next
to nothing   a thin grey powder   like salt

The Windscreen

Ice on the windscreen blocking your view
froze me out on the outside too.

Were you in there on the passenger side,
waiting, still along for the ride,

while I scraped at the glass with my nails?
I froze at the touch to learn how it feels

to have my view of you clouded over
as you disappeared behind this weather,

this terrible weather we've been having.
I sealed you in more, even just breathing.

I sprayed the de-icer and wiped the rag
over the crystals starting to crack

and streak to the bonnet gutter in tears,
until I broke through and you appeared,

and I was your St Bernard come
to haul you out and lead you home,

with a flask of brandy for your lips;
except my busy fingertips

could crack the ice but not the glass,
the only breath I felt was the car's

and we were leaving, not going home,
and no windscreen could shelter you from

this cold that was only getting worse,
and my lips stayed dry, and so did yours.

My Back Pages

I crossed the sea. Half my address book
blew away and never came back.

It's one way to weed the cabbage patch.
I never did like them all that much.

I stopped sending Christmas cards and letters.
The other half went. I never felt better.

Which left me and the takeaway man,
except when I got down to one

I wasn't so sure I made the cut
so mine was the page that I ripped out.

I'd decided I liked me less and less.
I'd done my throwing out in reverse.

I was the lack that I'd always lacked.
Get rid of me and you're all welcome back.

Ljubljana

Because I will never return
from that all-giving place

journey in my steps
to a city named 'beloved'.

Come join me there. Or don't come:
stay at home unless

you bring what you come for, love.
Come and bring all you have left.

Notes and Acknowledgements

Acknowledgement is gratefully made to the editors of *Agenda, The Backyards of Heaven* (Waterford Institute of Technology, 2003), *The Bend, College Green, De Brakke Hond, Dublin Review, Free Verse, Irish Pages, Irish University Review, The Irish Times, Irish Writers Against War* (O'Brien Press, 2003), *The Journal of Irish Studies* (Japan), *Matrix, The New Irish Poets* (Bloodaxe, 2004), *Poetry Ireland Review, Poetry Review, Poetry Wales, The Rooney Prize: A Celebration* (2002), *The SHOp, Thumbscrew, Times Literary Supplement, TriQuarterly, The Wake Forest Series of Irish Poetry vol. 1* (WFUP, 2005), *The Yellow Nib*, and the online anthology of the Irish Writers Centre. A selection of these poems appeared in the chapbook *Three-Legged Dog* with poems by Caitríona O'Reilly (Wild Honey Press, 2003).

'Stan' and 'Gable End' first appeared in *Poetry* (Chicago).

'Riptide', 'The Teardrop Explodes', 'St John and the Eagle', 'The Owl', 'Fintan and the Hawk of Achill' and 'Owls, Fort Paull' were written for an exhibition of words and images celebrating the birds of prey at Fort Paull, Hull, that appeared at the Hull Literature Festival, 2003.

'Whalebone Haiku' appeared on beer mats in the Whalebone pub, Hull, during the Hull Literature Festival, 2006. 'Cod Liver Oil' was one of a group of poems commissioned by Hull City Council to mark the unveiling of Steinunn Thórarinsdóttir's sculpture *Voyage* in June 2006.

for Caitríona